'Heaven is Real'
John Maus and
the Truth of Pop

Precinct

CONTENTS

Great art is always a mystery, a mixture of this world – a world we're familiar with – and something of the next. You could say that it has one foot on the Earth and one foot in Heaven – or indeed one foot in Hell or madness, depending on your preference. Great art takes us to a place that is between Earth and Utopia, between the 'real' and the 'unreal,' or a new Real. It shows us what we are and what we can become, and may even take us there in the process.

John Maus is a composer, performer, home-recording artist and philosopher from Minnesota, USA. Born in 1980, he earned fame in independent pop circles with his albums *Songs* (2006), *Love is Real* (2007) and *We Must Become the Pitiless Censors of Ourselves* (2011). Maus's project is a religiously ecstatic musical pilgrimage through Earth to Heaven and Hell, a believer's quest to reach the quintessence of pop's emotional and political expressivity, or else discover such a thing merely to be a starry-eyed mirage. For it's the ambiguity of Maus's Utopia that arguably makes it so compelling, so provocatively lost somewhere between Heaven and

Earth. The first track on *Love is Real* challenges us with the assertion in its title, 'Heaven is Real': has Maus brought us to a Heaven that is real, are we basking in the hope-giving glow of a Love that is real? Or do we feel the disillusionment of pop's quixotic project, the ironic permanence of earthly banality, even a Hell in which the joy of transcendence is hubris, punished, impossible and forever out of reach? For Maus's idiom is prosaically handmade, using hissing tapes and less-than-cutting-edge synthesizers; he is one of the pre-eminent 'lo-fi' practitioners of our time. His homemade rapture recalls those of the American 'outsider artists' who crept out of obscurity in the last decades of the twentieth century – Daniel Johnston, Henry Darger, Charles Ives, Wesley Willis, James Hampton, Hasil Adkins, Achilles Rizzoli. Yet outsiders are not what they once were: Maus is classically trained in music and a PhD-level reader of phil-osophy, versed in the work of Martin Heidegger and Alain Badiou. But just as in the almost-freakshows of the outsider artists, whether or not we discover that Heaven (or love, or truth, or togetherness) is real, or whether there is only the kitschy, idiosyncratic and undignified Hell on Earth of all-too-human venture, will be a matter of faith.

In any case, Maus certainly offers listeners a pop that draws a transcendent power from its elegant, well-crafted simplicity. His Romantic pop of shimmering synths undeniably brings out all the sweetness of a single chord progression, the momentum of an ostinato and the immediacy of a lyrical fragment, all entirely within the nobly 'savage', humanising and refreshingly personal context of home-recorded composition. Like those of his occasional collaborator and friend of over a decade Ariel Pink, and to a certain extent those of Pink's mentor R Stevie Moore, Maus's songs seem to dabble in what might traditionally be deemed to be kitsch and naïveté in the context of nostalgia, but such qualities aren't merely there for shallow thrills or cheap shots. Maus, Pink, Moore and an increasing number of like-minded musical auteurs are showing us 'pop about pop': a critical commentary on the mediation between personal and popular aesthetics for which the message is (in) the medium. Thus they collapse the sacred triptych of Earth, Heaven and Hell, showing us how they actually coexist simultaneously.

The metapop of Maus and Pink is constantly likened to the sounds of previous artists by music critics, a technique which doesn't do justice to their project, and their work is invariably described as 'nostalgic'. Notions of nostalgia, pastiche and reference have dominated writing on recent trends in musical aesthetics, frequently in a mood of frustration, and games of association have become particularly popular. Such a way of imagining and approaching new music only prescribes and ossifies listening. Besides, a diagnosis of 'nostalgia' in art is often a futurist opinion, only conceivable from the viewpoint of an aesthetic agenda built around an imperative toward the wholly new. Any partial return to or resonance of old methods – that is, an established Earth from which to begin one's journey – is only 'backward-looking' in the eyes of a doctrine that demands a progress predicated upon the constant invention of new (ie believed to be radically unfamiliar) methods. An alternative, more finely tuned conception of progress sees the interaction of past and present in the formulation of increasingly subtle artistic results in a favourable light, as enriching and fertilising the present with the de- (and re-) familiarisation of the past.

Such balance between the 'old/familiar' and the 'new/unfamiliar' is of course an example of the Earth vs Utopia aesthetic described above. So in many cases we might see 'nostalgia's' pining for its given utopias as a fruitful aesthetic strategy, and actually this is one of the central tenets of Romantic aesthetics, as Romantic art projects Heavens or Hells onto 'reality' for emotionally resonant or fantastical effect. If romanticism does this and otherwise prioritises emotional resonance over other potential aesthetic concerns, it's conceivably not restricted to nineteenth-century art and criticism, as is often believed. Though John Maus's musical idiom can only occasionally be reduced to pastiche, a major component of his utopian vision of Heaven is its resonance with eighties synth pop and film/television soundtracks. To twentieth-

century ears, this era's pure and confi-
dently expressed sentimentality often
reappears as kitsch, or is appreciated
with a degree of irony. Treating this or
any subject matter with lo-fi framing
effects (ie incorporating, as Maus does,
tape hiss, crackly, over-saturated volumes,
attenuated high frequencies and various
other 'unprofessional' symptoms, or
procedures such as collage) can sanitise
these sentiments by coating them in a
layer of irony that manifests either within
the work or, ultimately, as a result of its
historical context. These effects remind
us that we and the artist 'know' the music
being framed to be anachronistic and
aesthetically invalid, thus saving us from
the bad taste of what has rotten and been
discarded. This irony can be by turns
tragic, melancholic, playful, bitter, dis-
turbing or satirical – all shades that seem
to appear in Maus's work.

John Maus is much more than this however, and when it comes to the potential for
irony his music is intriguingly ambiguous.
Ariel Pink put it this way, strongly denying
that irony is a factor in Maus's aesthetic by
emphasizing its opposite, sincerity:

John Maus is a maniac on a bloody crusade – a tortured evangelist on a mercenary quest to rid our world of villainous defilers of The Gospel of True Love. By turns shockingly infectious and disarmingly unpredictable, his music conflates a perplexing marriage of Moroder's 'Never Ending Story' and classical 12-tone renegades of 20th century past, harking the new path which resurrects romance from its post-modern shackles, and reignites the promise of a better world.

But then maybe Pink is in on the irony – does he really believe in a 'Gospel of True Love'? Maus's own words suggest a more complex relationship with what an observer might call irony, or as Pink put it, postmodernity. In a video interview with *XLR8R* magazine, Maus emphasises that he's 'not trying to say that there's such a thing as sincerity or authenticity', though he still believes in arriving at a genuine communality and that the task of music is to 'connect' with audiences: 'it's about being with each other'.

Maus's essay and interview on
R Stevie Moore's website reveal a great
deal more about how he believes a listener might reconcile notions of irony
and 'truth' (though he never actually
uses the word 'irony' in connection with
music). They present sophisticated theo-
ries about his own music and that of
Moore and Pink that show the influence
of Badiou, particularly his concept of
the 'truth procedure' – a process through
which truth is presented in a discursive
context, such as Art. Maus believes that
Moore and Pink 'proceed towards the
singular truth of pop' through the 'excessive affirmation' of the 'particulars of
pop', namely 'standardization, materializa-
tion and multiplication'. To quote haphaz-
ardly from Maus's methodical and
meticulous essay:

> *R Stevie and Ariel… exceed the stand-
> ardization of pop through excessive
> affirmation of this particular in all of its
> own particulars: standardization of
> form, standardized emotional intention,
> standardization of genre, and so on.
> Standardization of form is the commod-*

ification of what listeners listen to in the way called music, that it will meet particular standards: song form, tonality, periodic rhythm, and so on. In the pop song 'You Are True', R Stevie exceeds standardization of form though affirmation of it, ie, this pop song is too much a pop song... This affirmation exceeds what there is. In it, the untruth of the situation becomes obvious not through negation, which commercial capitalism can always appropriate and thus even solicits, but through excessive affirmation ie subjective expression of what there is.

...R Stevie and Ariel exceed an untrue situational state where everyone is 'self-evidently equal' and therefore 'replaceable,' such an affirmation of subjectivity is truthful. Moreover, this affirmation is the progressive purification of pop towards its truth through the subtraction of genre.

Maus also addresses the lo-fi qualities, or 'the materiality' of the 'obsolete', in Moore and Pink's recordings – again as an 'excessive affirmation' of pop's truth:

*...Materialization of pop means, eg,
pop as consumable object, the pop
record album's inextricability from the
materials of its production, and so
on... R Stevie and Ariel use production
materials in all of their manifestations,
not only those currently in fashion.
As the situational state continues to
'improve' its means of production, ie,
through new products and planned
obsolescence, the use of now obsolete
materials speaks to something in excess
of it. Moreover, R Stevie and Ariel
foreground the materiality of these
obsolete materials.*

It could be appropriate to consider this
'excessive affirmation' that 'speaks to
untruth' as having an ironic, sarcastic,
satirical dimension. And yet it certainly
isn't clear that Moore, Pink and Maus
consider 'the truth of pop' in negative
terms, or that their music is merely a
satirical drawing back of the veil to reveal
ugliness beneath. On the contrary, all
three artists seem in love with 'the truth
of pop', and each of them has shown
us genuine moments of transcendent

sweetness. But perhaps this is an irony that doesn't require a sneering cynicism. The most emphatic exploration of the nature of pop's truth is in Maus's (and Pink's) music, which forces us to consider whether pop is shown to be the commodified sham of a hellish musical dystopia (through irony), or a touchingly, amusingly earthy effort – or real, true and heavenly. The liberating genius of Maus and Pink is that in their music all three of these apparently contradictory readings are ambiguously and inextricably presentable. We 'proceed', as on a journey, to this conclusion, an apparent contradiction in terms that points to a perfect truth about art.

PERFECT IMPERFECTION

In a statement influenced by the nineteenth-century transcendental philosophy of Ralph Waldo Emerson, the American musical pioneer Charles Ives, who ninety years before had a very similar artistic project to Pink and Maus, asserted that 'vagueness is at times an indication of nearness to a perfect truth'. The vagueness of truth and truth of vagueness are perfected in Maus's music.

On *Love is Real* this is apparent from the opening, 'Heaven is Real'. The statements 'love is real' and 'heaven is real' imply a rejoinder, so the fact that Maus has felt the need to make them could introduce doubt about their veracity. These titles respond to a cultural context in which as opinions they're denied and disbelieved – not everyone would take such statements at face value in a postmodern climate. With an almost heartbreaking sincerity, the lyrics of 'Heaven is Real' promise us that 'you don't have to run away from love any more', adding 'that's what friends and love is for / love the world and love all man'. And yet as in a Lied by Schubert or Schumann that sets a Heinrich Heine poem, it's artfully unclear whether the musical accompaniment is in agreement with these lyrics, potentially naïve (in a Romantically ironic way) as they are (note that in the *XLR8R* interview, Maus quotes that 'the worst thing that ever happened to music was words'). The harmonic feel is minor, the tempo high, the voice acoustically distant, the chords evasively syncopated and the overall mood one of anxious, fleet-footed uncertainty – we don't feel safe, certainly not as safe as we might do in *Songs'* 'Through the Skies For You' or *Pitiless Censors'* 'Believer'. Are we still running from love, despite the lyrics? Is Maus's fatherly, Christ-like voice calling after us with wise advice, attempting to sooth us as we continue to flee? Does he succeed? Which is 'true', the words or the music? There are no answers or resolutions – in fact, the dimly-heard lyrics of the chorus seem to alternate between telling us 'run away' and 'don't run away'.

It doesn't always take an apparent clash between the lyrics and the musical accompaniment to hint at imperfection. Maus's lyrics are often in themselves perfectly poised between the genuinely persuasive and the ironically unpersuasive. This balance is often achieved because the lyrics for each song are typically little more than a phrase or sentence or two, a slogan, repeated 'excessively'. In the *XLR8R* interview, Maus notes that his brother calls these slogans the 'mantras' in his songs. The apparent seriousness with which they're delivered in Maus's booming baritone over and over, and over, again is immediately amusing, but this fades into an ambiguous sincerity as the singer battles to emphasise a point which is becoming both clearer and more perplexing over time. On *Songs* the mantras are more likely to be taken as comically offbeat especially in the context of a song: 'it's time to die', 'it's time to get a job', 'such a maniac', 'less talk more action', 'no-one loves a cowgirl'. On *Love is Real* and *Pitiless Censors* the mantras seem, on some level, to become more morally or politically aware: 'too much money', 'don't worship the devil', 'times is weird', 'cop killer', 'pussy is not a matter of fact'.

One of the most memorable mantras in Maus's music is the eponymous 'Rights for Gays', in which the only elaboration or argument in support of this vague political slogan, which is repeated 12 times, is 'oh yeah'. Maus then goes onto further demand 'medical care for everyone,' imagining that 'the doctor is in'. The song is bound to amuse, and yet it cannot be denied that the phrase 'Rights for Gays' is a valid, powerful sentiment rooted in decades of historical struggle. It's difficult to accept that there is no self-awareness (perhaps irony, if you like) whatsoever about the simplicity or naïveté of 'Rights for Gays' as a politically active song. So ultimately 'Rights for Gays' could be taken as a woefully, tragically inadequate attempt at articulating a political statement (Hell), an homage to conventional, everyday politics (Earth) or a heroic demand for a more utopian society (Heaven). It's all three simultaneously. Similarly, 'pussy is not a matter of fact' on *Pitiless Censors* is a statement with a vague feminist persuasiveness, but doesn't have any qualifying statements. Is the term 'pussy' to be taken in an anatomical or a potentially sexist socio-cultural sense? What does 'not a matter of fact' mean – not pragmatic or not real? And not a 'matter of fact' for whom? If we are journeying towards truth and a perfect society with a Utopian approach to gender, Maus's discursive imperfection seems to remind us that we're not quite there yet, and that we should struggle on.

Another potential symbol of utopian perfection that's introduced and then 'imperfected' in Maus's work is classical counterpoint. Developed in the Medieval era, counterpoint is a set of rules and practices concerning how multiple vocal or instrumental parts best interact in polyphonic music to create pleasing harmony and rhythmic structure. Maus has shown not only extensive knowledge of the traditions and disciplines of this musical art – particularly as it pertains to choral music from the beginnings of polyphony through the Medieval, Renaissance and Baroque eras to Brahms – but proficiency in it too, with passages of counterpoint appearing in all of his albums. That Maus is an expert in the (now unfortunately largely anachronistic) techniques of counterpoint makes him a Luke Skywalker-like figure, the only Jedi of his generation, born and trained in their age-old arts after their demise, the brave new hope for defeating the evil Empire of pop music's compositional sloth. Actually there are more than a few students of counterpoint today, but there can't be many who bring the craft directly into

the field of pop like Maus does. One
of the tracks on *Love is Real*, 'Green
Bouzard', is a brilliantly executed tradi-
tional fugal passage in the style of Handel
or Bach, whose skill at counterpoint is
frequently seen as representing a spiritual
'perfection'. This fugue is hardly presented in the most perfect of circumstances
however – the sound quality is low, it's
played on the somewhat cheesy imitation
pipe organ voice of an electronic key-
board, and at the very beginning the
reverb tails from some now cut previous
notes still linger. In these ways the piece
hints at unprofessionality, even kitsch,
and yet at the same time the mastery
of the fugue remains – Earth, Hell and
Heaven seem one.

Counterpoint also appears in *Songs*'
'Real Bad Job' where its diligence seems
to represent looking for, getting or doing
a job in sharp contrast to the downtempo,
downtrodden surrounding material,
which whines that 'it's time to get a job'.
It's a major aspect of *Love is Real*'s 'Love
Letters from Hell' too. In this complex
song, Maus appropriates the musical
material of the song from the Agnus Dei

of the Missa La Sol Fa Re Mi by revered
fifteenth- and sixteenth-century master
of sacred polyphony Josquin des Prez.
The combination of pop and a Renaissance mass section is smoothly done,
and the lyrics of the song work together
with the liturgical text of the Agnus Dei:
'Lamb of God, who takest away the sin
of the world, have mercy upon us... grant
us peace (Agnus Dei, qui tollis peccata
mundi, miserere nobis... dona nobis
pacem)'. Note that 'the world' is the bear-
er of sin. Maus's lyrics are thematically
in parallel, much like the countermelodies
of counterpoint:

> *I'm feeling very sorry that it hasn't*
> > *rained all year*
> *I'm feeling very sorry, and I've got*
> > *the fear*
> *It's taking time to sort through my*
> > *winding mind*
> *While they are tortured on my watch*
> *We've got to find a way*
> *Don't let them fade away, baby*
> *We've got to change the way*
> *'Til there's no one left inside this*
> > *secret place.*

The traditionally pop-like lyrics ('baby') hint at sins of omission, a subsequent guilt and the need for a redemptive journey ('way') while the text implied by the setting of Josquin's aesthetically and religiously sacred Agnus Dei offers absolution. The combination of words that suggest a Hell or a Purgatory with Heaven's comforting, forgiving music proceeding us towards it. But is pop made sacred and heavenly here, or is sacred Renaissance counterpoint brought down to earth, made hellish? Is the combination of the two a folly or a utopian gesture? Again, we are left only with faith.

BAROQUE EXCESS

More than one commentator has described Maus's music as 'baroque pop'. Although the inclusion of a Handelian fugue makes the definition rather literal in Maus's case, the term 'baroque pop' has always seemed quite vague and a little misplaced. It traditionally describes the mid-sixties pop that incorporated classical instrumentation, and the fact

that the most prominent of these instruments was often the harpsichord probably
went some way in suggesting the epithet
'baroque', though the musical style is
rarely akin to the classically 'baroque'
music of the seventeenth and early eight-
eenth centuries. Although Maus's work
often has the dramatic and Romantic
qualities of sixties baroque pop, it can't
be said to have its characteristic instrumentation or formal structures.

   Actually the word 'baroque' refers to
a deformed or irregularly-shaped pearl,
which already seems, with its ironic mixture of the traditionally 'beautiful' and
the traditionally 'flawed' or 'low quality',
a suitable metaphor for Maus's music.
The word was first applied to music in
1733 to disparagingly describe Rameau's
opera *Hippolyte et Aricie*, being used then
and subsequently as a generally pejorative
term describing bizarre, extravagant,
excessively aesthetic or aesthetically
distasteful or unprofessional music before
it later became the name for an era in
Western classical music. In other words,
'baroque' music is kitsch, camp, 'over
the top'. Again, this definition is perhaps

appropriate given the differential between Maus's work and today's mainstream pop. This aesthetic of 'excess' – 'excessive affirmation' – was of course established in Maus's essay to describe the songs of Moore and Pink as allowing these artists and Maus to 'proceed towards the truth of pop'. By the standards of today's pop mainstream, Maus's voice alone has certain negatively 'baroque', 'over-the-top' qualities, both poetically and sonically. It's often 'too deep' or 'too resonant' for the fashions of today's mainstream pop, and the faux-English accent and the pronunciation of words like 'baby' and 'town' (in 'Old Town' on *Love is Real*) is 'affected' and 'over-stylised' – all qualities that can be attractive in themselves of course. As poetic, Romantic utterances Maus's songs are similarly 'baroque', perhaps none more so than on *Love is Real*'s 'The Silent Chorus'. The text of this song alternates between and mixes together various Heavens and Hells, it's both deeply Romantic (potentially to excess) and descriptive of nostalgic sentiment:

This is the time for all but sunset
And this is the time to hang our sorrows
up in cedar trees
This is the time to gather at tables aloud
with memory
Of our lost play and childish pageantry

This is the time for lost abandonment
And this is the time for stupid whores
and drunken malady
For th'earning keep through joyless
drudgery

La la la la la, (etc)

Note that in the *XLR8R* interview Maus
tells us that while he was writing *Love is
Real* he was working as a cable guy! As
a backdrop for these undeniably poignant
lyrics, Maus lays down one of the most
sublimely beautiful soundscapes on
the album – warm synths guided through
monumental chord progressions are
layered like clouds at sunset, guitars tingle
like the strumming of angels' harps,
divine drums echo across an enormous
space and minor resolves constantly into
major as the pearly gates slowly open to

bathe us in rays of transfiguring light.

Perhaps the 'excess' and 'imperfection' in 'The Silent Chorus' illustrates a truer or more aesthetically final pop than those from the apparently less self-aware tradition of comparable transfiguration songs by the nineteen-eighties Romantic pop heroes Maus is often compared to, such as Scott Walker and Joy Division etc (ie Walker's 'The Electrician' etc, Joy Division's 'Atmosphere' etc, even songs like Phil Collins's 'Take Me Home' etc). This transfiguration song is too much a transfiguration song. Indeed, reviewing in *The Wire*, Simon Hampson noted that 'with its theatrical mid-Atlantic baritone and icy synth textures, *Love is Real* sometimes recalls late Joy Division, albeit with a greater self-awareness about how camp such miserabilism can be.' By rising above inevitably changeable pop aesthetics, rooted as they are in relativism, shifting fashions and an indecisive discourse on music for which all that was ever worthy eventually turns to kitsch or becomes negatively 'baroque' anyway, Maus begins to reach 'the truth of pop' as it's relevant today.

One of the most memorable moments of excess on *Love is Real* happens at the centre of the album, in 'Tenebrae'. By all accounts 'Tenebrae' is a religious observance that takes its name from the services celebrated by Catholics and some Protestants during Holy Week, hence its mantra, 'sing to the mystery of his blood'. The first section connotes church music and perhaps plainchant, then follows a section of classical counterpoint derived from the opening material. Suddenly a third section arrives with enormously thick, awe-inspiring chord sequences. This section is excessive and 'over the top' in a quite literal, sonic sense because it exceeds headroom (the maximum volume allowable by the technology) and thus becomes crackly and indistinct. More-over, the beginning of this third section has been utterly unprepared for. Normally in a similar work by a Romantic composer such as Brahms or Mahler this climactic moment would have been prepared for by a textural and dynamic crescendo at least several minutes long, but here it enters unannounced at full volume, right at a metrically unstressed

part of the counterpoint. Such an intro-
duction satisfies the eighteenth-century
pejorative definition of 'baroque', but
it can be seen as a masterstroke – just
as religious faith is tested, it tests one's
aesthetic faith.

It could also be seen to represent the
Passion with more immediacy and reality
(truth) than a more aesthetically re-
strained style might have. There is a key
part of the Tenebrae celebrations, the
strepitus ('great noise'), in which a loud
noise is made by some means (such as
slamming a book) while the church is in
complete darkness, an act which symbol-
ises the earthquake that followed the
death of Christ. The entry of Maus's own
noisy strepitus surprises the listener in
a similar fashion, and aptly portrays the
awesome power of the earthquake (and
the similarly awesome power of the Lord
God), making a decidedly 'great noise'
in the process. 'Tenebrae' is followed by
the song 'Too Much Money', where a similar event occurs: its mantra asks 'whatcha
gonna do with all that money?' until
suddenly halfway through the song there's
an almost deafening scream. This shock-

ing, hellish moment of pain obscures the music entirely and pushes the listener's 'aesthetic faith' to the very limit. As such it recalls the biblical promise that judgment day will come 'like a thief in the night', and as Christ said, 'I tell you the truth, it is hard for a rich man to enter the kingdom of heaven. Again I tell you, it is easier for a camel to go through the eye of a needle than for a rich man to enter the kingdom of God'.

AND HIS KINGDOM WAS PLUNGED INTO DARKNESS

'Too Much Money' is just one of many apocalyptic or purgatorial moments in Maus's work. Another, and one of the most oddly beguiling, is 'Pure Rockets', also on *Love is Real*. Its text is minimal:

> *Missiles in flight*
> *Oh no*
> *Time to say goodbye to the sky*
> *Time to say goodbye to the trees and*
>   *the oceans and the breezes*
> *Missiles are headed towards your house*

The disjunction between this text and the gorgeous eventual resolutions to major harmony that are so characteristic of Maus's more recent work – and seem to express such hope and happiness – is chilling, and chillingly liberating. Evidently this song constitutes the two-minute warning prior to oblivion, and the lyrical message is child-like and simple. It's the chorus that really raises the hairs on the back of the neck: a low-pass filter is applied to cut off the higher frequencies the synths, muffling them and making them seem distant, dreamlike, wistful and elegiac; the chords they enact are airy second inversion triads, often syncopated. It's as if we're spotting contrails in the upper atmosphere or witnessing explosive impacts that will turn into mushroom clouds on the horizon. The phrase 'missiles in flight' is emphasised overall, the enduring image constantly reiterated in different decorative permutations and magnified by time-stretching, obsessively scrutinised like the idée fixe of some trauma-induced psychosis. This Armageddon is undeniably sweet, and yet somehow this sweetness doesn't seem inappropriate enough to allow us to dismiss it as a simple irony. 'Pure Rockets' makes the subject of imminent Hell on Earth into a Heaven.

Maus also envisions the cleansing, redemptive dream of Heaven engulfing the sin and weakness of worldly material in the aptly titled 'The Peace That Earth Cannot Bring' on *Songs*, which assures us that 'soon this world will be over' to a genial disco beat. 'I'm stuck inside this flesh, this painful, scary flesh... worthless flesh,' Maus then confesses, before assuring us that we can 'break through the madness of the night.' In fact, like a Romantic symphony, *We Must Become the Pitiless Censors of Ourselves* is itself an epic journey from light to deep darkness and back into the light. On the record's cover is a relatively kitschy image of a lighthouse emitting a beam of light from its warm yellow bulb amid the dark blue of a stormy night – the sort of picture that would appear on a corporate motivational poster. Yet once again Maus's struggle towards the light is far from insincere or cynical.

The album begins with the comparatively serene 'Streetlight' and the celebratory 'Quantum Leap', which exults in how 'we are the ones who seem to travel through time'. Then, however, adversity strikes in the Noah's Flood deluge of 'And the Rain', where Maus's distant voice promises that 'someone is telling the truth' before lightning strikes across the tom-toms and timbres and harmonies reminiscent of 'Pure Rockets' support the mantra 'and the rain came down, down, down, down.' At the mid-point of the album is the encouragement of 'Keep Pushing On', where Maus's even more distant voice echoes from all directions in the fog of tape hiss, urging us onward with the eponymous mantra. Despite its catchy refrain and strong beat, the track isn't the dance anthem it has the potential to be – as its title suggest, it still has some way to go.

Then comes a vision of the Cross in 'The Crucifix', turning sacred, chanted melodies into a grimly effect dance groove – is it a source of holy encouragement for us pilgrims or a setback, a vision of human sin and cruelty and the nadir of the Messiah's time on Earth? Next, the Babylonian dancefloor of 'Head for the

Country' is the closest Maus has ever
got to a pastiche of nineteen-eighties pop.
Here it's early electro disco circa 1983,
falteringly stuffed with many different
pompous riffs that support lyrics such as
'this is where the human being finds itself,
in the locker' and 'somewhere there's
a crime being committed'. This latter
statement anticipates the following track,
'Cop Killer' whose comically blatant
mantra 'cop killer, let's kill the cops to-
night… against the law' is at odds with
its slow and grandiose accompaniment.
'Cop Killer' contains what is perhaps
Maus's most morally reprehensible mantra, yet the emotional depth of the music
is such that we can't dismiss it as irony.
And whose side are these cops on here?
Are they angels, the upholders of social
peace and the law, that are to be killed?
Or are they devils, 'the pigs', 'the filth',
the violent, fascist arm of the state, to be
exterminated for the greater good? Mired
in relativism, it's an episode of deep
moral confusion and guilt.

As *Pitiless Censors* goes on, its songs
become even more bizarre and baroque.
The brutal declarations of 'Matter of Fact'

are preceded by electronically simulated thunder and lightning and more holy chord progressions, harking back to *Love is Real*'s 'Tenebrae'. Perhaps in the context of the album's arc, the word 'pussy' takes on a different meaning – a coward – and this song's mantra 'pussy is not a matter of fact' is just a roundabout, mentally hindered way of saying 'I am not afraid'. The night is darkest before the dawn, and the penultimate track 'We Can Break Through', whose title is almost synonymous with 'Keep Pushing On', is the album's most challenging moment. The beat is irregular and unpredictable, the snaking synths tortuous, the melodic sensibility exhausted and the voice is deep and fragmented as it intones, 'the night is calling us' and 'we can break through this'. The album's final track, its dawn, is 'Believer', with Maus following one of his most complex and least stable songs with one of his simplest and most stable. The bass guitar spends most of its time emphasising the tonic of the home key, visiting only the traditionally close chords IV and V. The chorus arrives like the sun when a dominant seventh resolves back into the home key, over which Maus announces, 'they call me the believer'. Bells ring, the air glistens with synth – we've made it.

Or have we? Is this Heaven? Can the transfiguration of 'Believer' really be taken at face value? Note that at the moment of vindication, the beginning of the song's chorus, the words are 'they call me the believer'. Firstly, why has the 'we' of 'Quantum Leap' been reduced to the subjectivity of 'me'? Why is it not 'we are the believers'? Is Maus no longer able to speak for anyone but himself? Secondly, why 'call' someone a believer, why not say 'I am the believer'? If the voice is merely 'called' a believer, that has left some significant room for doubt. Thirdly, why merely a 'believer', why have we stopped at mere 'belief'? Is the ostensible victory of 'Believer' not a real, concrete, matter of fact? Do we only 'believe' we have succeeded? Are we, in fact, still struggling in an all-too-human purgatory, where there is only belief and not certain truth? The words that follow in the bar after 'they call me the believer' are at best indistinct, and at worst not words at all but animal barks. Is this inarticulacy an idiolectic curse of the human condition, or is it 'speaking in tongues', the transcendence of earthly meaning?

With the statement 'they call me the believer', Maus seems to be giving a semi-apologetic account of himself as a subject of the admiration or derision (which is it?) of others. No longer are 'we' alongside Maus, but we are witnessing him through the eyes of others. This is borne out in the video to the song, where we see Maus calmly sat in profile, and we watch him rather than converse with him. Or is 'they call me the believer' an ironic understatement? Is it more modest, more suave – more convincing – to quote the opinions of others rather than be straightforwardly boastful? It leaves room for a final test of faith, reminding us that we will always be striving towards the Heaven we believe, and that this belief is, itself, heavenly redemption.

So is Heaven real? That'll depend on the faith of Maus's listeners, like the parable of Carl Theodore Dreyer's film *Ordet*, in which an apparent madman who claims he is Christ is faithlessly disbelieved by even the most zealous of religious believers on the grounds of the 'truth' of modern medical knowledge (replace that with 'contemporary aesthetic mores' for Maus's own gospel). Yet even the most icy-hearted and nihilistic listeners would find it difficult to resist being seduced on some level by the various Heavens Maus paints, to whatever extent they're understood ironically or not. One might conclude that Heaven is as real as its image and its effect on reality, both of which can certainly be felt in Maus's music. The final truth is that there is no single way of appreciating any art, and Maus demonstrates this truth for any and every listener by artfully rendering his music as aesthetically ambiguous and yet undeniably genuine. Ultimately it doesn't matter whether Heaven is real – because somewhere between Hell, Earth and Heaven (wherever they are, real or otherwise), John Maus believes in the truth of pop, and he is finding it.

Adam Harper is researching for a PhD in home-recorded, 'lo-fi' popular music. His music criticism blog Rouge's Foam has seen essays on subjects such as microrhythm and pitchbending in contemporary dance music and the framing of nostalgia in electronic music. He has written for Wire *magazine and is the author of* Infinite Music: Imagining the Next Millennium of Human Music-Making *(Zero Books, 2011).*

An earlier version of this essay was originally published on 4 July 2009 at www.rougesfoam.blogspot.com

Interview with John Maus

By Wayne Daly
& Grégory Ambos
21 April 2011

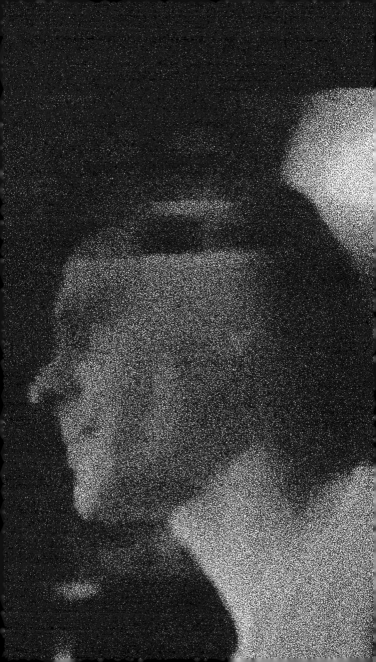

WD/GA: Could you discuss some of the themes on *We Must Become the Pitiless Censors of Ourselves*?

JM: The album is about the struggle to keep going, to keep pushing on, and endlessly so, towards the impossible. I wish I had a better language, but unfortunately, this old fashioned one is all I have: we want a different, better world. In the work, what I'm trying at, then, is a singular anticipation of what would finally be itself.

WD/GA: The album title is a declamation of intent, a clarion call. Who or what are you addressing?

JM: All of us, I guess, or, at least, any of us consciously engaged in so-called 'creative' activity. The idea is, of course, that in a situation where seemingly everything is encouraged and permitted, the only way we can truly appear is as the pitiless censors of ourselves: towards that about us which is never permitted, you know?, from the standpoint of our situation.

49

Now, I know many people think it's a stupid error to believe we are anything else than how we appear, but, for my own part, I can't help but suspect we are potentially more, and infinitely so. The imperative upon us then, as it has seemed to me, is infinite convergence upon that pure potentiality.

WD/GA: For the most part there is a staunch autonomy about your work. What is at stake for you in choosing to work this way?

JM: Again, in the absence of a better language, what I suspect is at stake working the way I have has to do with the old fashion distinction between potentiality and actuality. That is, any actuality which would put us to work towards an end other than each other, that is, towards itself instead of towards what we might potentially become, is a movement in the wrong direction. The right direction, so far as I can tell, and as I just said above, would be singularly and endlessly *through* these re-presentations towards each other in the element of our pure presentation. All this is very naïve of me, I know, and very much a privileged conceit part and parcel with my own cultural situation as a middle-class, white, male. Even still, and no matter how naïve or convenient it is for me to say so, I suspect we are something else than the generalities knowledge would have us suppose we are. There is a better world than the one discourse presently constitutes: the world disclosed when each of us singularly wrest ourselves *through* discourse as *something else than* discourse.

WD/GA: The new album includes a hypnotic reworking of Molly Nilsson's 'Hey Moon!'. How did the duet transpire?

JM: Molly and I were 'friends' on the computer, she sent me the song and it really resonated with me. You see, at the time, I was up all night, alone in my office, working on music, so I felt like I really understood what that song was after. More importantly than this, I suppose, is the mileage she seemed to wrest out of a very conventional harmonic idea – a hallmark of true pop music. I took her track, mixed it up a little bit, and added my voice and some instruments.

WD/GA: Your live shows are something to behold; the times I've seen you in London have been heightened experiences. What is the live performance like for you? What's going through your mind when you're on stage?

JM: I think it is a misfortune of our world, perhaps of any world, that so few places, and always only, of course, in the strictest and most tightly controlled way, are provided for us to try and appear as we potentially can. Here I am going on again about 'appearing as we are', but please, grant me this much, that I would never suppose this is about being authentic or something like that. On the contrary, on these 'stages', the way we appear is precisely as a singular manipulation of the general, always inauthentically, of course, but in a singular way. Up on the 'stage', and despite the bad complicity necessarily involved in getting up there, I am confronted with the same impossibility that I am when I sit down to the work: to try and appear as something else, something singularly non-identical with the untruth. Particularly, my wager has always been that the 'hysterical body is exemplary in its affirmation'. Although, I am not sure I will be able to continue doing this, for obvious reasons.

WD/GA: What are you reading at the moment? Are there writers that have a notable influence on your own writing and lyrics?

JM: Maybe I could use this question instead as a chance to ask anyone reading my answer for help, because I read a lot of old people, you know?, old people and dead people, and they certainly speak to me, but what they

53

say comes at me as if from another situation. It seems they use a language with conventions and presuppositions that are particular to another situation than mine. They talk about things like the 'night of the world' and the 'default of the gods', which is fine, of course, but they talk about all this using their language. They talk about Mallarmé and Beckett, Wagner and Schoenberg, and perhaps we should as well, but they never do this along-side punk rock. Please do not think I am merely asking after the gauntlet thrown down already by cultural studies departments everywhere, because I am not. What I'd like to see articulated is a thought capable of rising to our time, for we must always remember what Mouth said to us at the bottom of the Moss Garden wish-ing well: *it is our time down here.* Now, if that sounds stupid, or as if it were meant to be said tongue in cheek, then I apologise, because I do not mean it that way. The bottom line is, yes, I could go on about the old peo-ple, all of whom, to my mind at least, singularly rose to their own epochs. What I'd rather do, however, is make an open call: let us all rise, each time singularly, to our own epoch, that we might share ourselves with these and more as singular expressions of this particular world, 'the night of nights' as they might call it, let us give ourselves as so many neon icons in that night. Let us share with them and those to come how singular experience continued after the 'triumph of the spectacle', even if more hidden and more difficult than ever to wrest. We owe it to those old and dead, don't we?, who give us so much of themselves, of the experience of human beings in those particular worlds.

Conducted by email for
The What Where When
www.thewhatwherewhen.org

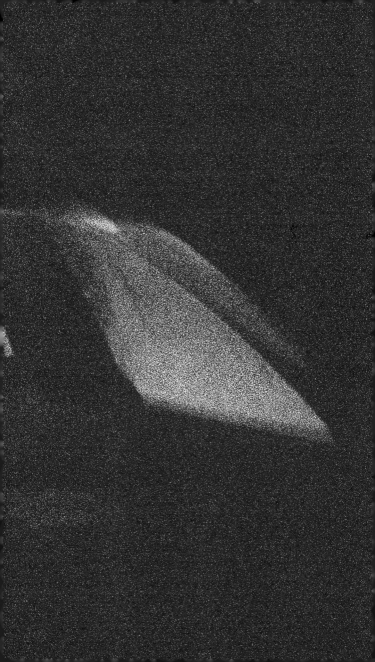

JOHN MAUS DISCOGRAPHY

Albums
2006: *Songs* (Upset the Rhythm)
2007: *Love is Real* (Upset the Rhythm)
2011: *We Must Become the Pitiless Censors
of Ourselves* (Upset the Rhythm)

Compilations
2011: *Rarities for Rough Trade* (Rough Trade)
2012: *A Collection of Rarities and Previously
Unreleased Material* (Ribbon Music)

Singles
2011: *Quantum Leap* (Upset the Rhythm)

Mix discs
2011: *Maus Mix* (Rough Trade)

Compilation Appearances
2006: *From US to I* (Ballbearings Pinatas)
2006: *The Human Ear* Vol 1
(Human Ear Music)
2007: *Mistletonia* (Mistletone)

With Ariel Pink
1999: *Underground* (Vinyl International)
2002: *Loverboy* (Ballbearings Pinatas)

Underground Releases
1991: *The Janitor's First LP*
  with Sam Anderson and Cory Boik
1992: *The Janitor's Second LP*
  with Sam Anderson and Cory Boik
1993: *A Janitor's EP*
  with Sam Anderson and Cory Boik
1994: *Early Songs 1*, with Cory Boik
1995: *Early Songs 2*
1996: *Early Songs 3*
1997: *Early Songs 4*
1998: *Mass Appeal*
  with the Tony Alonso Ensemble
1998: *The Mystery Molasses LP*
  with Ian Stahl, Jay Jensen,
  Gabe Schlocke and Jess Bednar
1998: *Early Songs 5*
2000: *Fish With Broken Dreams*
2001: *Snowless Winters EP*
2003: *I Want to Live*
2005: *Love Letters From Hell*

ACKNOWLEDGEMENTS

Grégory Ambos
Sophia Ben Yedder
Eleanor Brown at X Marks the Bökship
Lisa Durrant at In House Press
Claire McManus
Upset the Rhythm

IMAGE CREDITS

Believer, 2011, by Nicolas Amato,
John Maus and Jennifer Juniper Stratford

Do Your Best, 2007, director unknown

Maniac, 2006, by Emily Kuntz with
John Maus, Gab Danon and Janet Kim

Head For The Country, 2011
By Jennifer Juniper Stratford

Live photos by Wayne Daly:
The Rest is Noise, Brixton, 28 October 2009

Back cover: Park Nights at the Serpentine
Gallery, 6 August 2010

COLOPHON

'*Heaven Is Real*'
John Maus and the Truth of Pop
By Adam Harper

Design: Wayne Daly
Printed in England

ISBN: 978-0-9569524-0-0

Reprinted 2013

Also available as an ebook for
Amazon Kindle and Apple iBooks
eISBN: 978-0-9569524-4-8

Published by Precinct, London
www.precinct.cc
circulate@precinct.cc

'Up on the "stage"… I am confronted with the same impossibility that I am when I sit down to the work: to try and appear as something else, something singularly non-identical with the untruth.'